Love Tears an Mistletoe Years

*Love an
Tears &
Mistletoe
Years*

35 Poems By John Normanton

JOHN NORMANTON

Love Tears an Mistletoe Years

ISBN: 9798466816402

DEDICATION

I Dedicate this book to all it may affect and I hope you get
enjoyment in reading it, as I did writing it

CONTENTS

1

To Smile again

A smile upon your face each day

Is what we need, is what we pray

Our eyes are all, that we all see

to see that smile, to smile at me

To smile again will shine a light

To make us happy, happy and bright

To smile once more, can only be

To smile again

For you all to see.

Please, let's all smile again

2

Always together

It's been a while, we've been together

The love in us, shall live forever

It's been a while, a while in time

You are so sweet, so warm & kind

It's been a while, since we first met

A time in love, will never forget

It's been a while, a while to see

That I love you, and you love me

It's been a while, of love and sun

Of which I say you are the one

It's been a while,

as skies are blue To say to you,
I do love you

3

Falling tears

When a tear, falls from my face

It disappears without trace

And with some tear's that do not weep

Some are Tears, oh so deep

And with each hit's the ground

It cry's out, with a sound

The sound it makes is no disgrace

As it falls from your face.

4

Father's day

On this special day we have

We love you fathers, we love you dad

This is a day that fathers say

We need a rest we need to play

With the day so full of joy

Love from each girl & boy

Because we know

this goes without say

They are the best in everyway

We love you Fathers.

5

Hope

Hope is a dream we all wish for

To start the year to a brand new door

The door we open is not a dream

But a brand new year we've not yet seen?

And with this year is about to begin

In this life we have not seen

We have the time we live and cope

We live our life we live in hope

I hope next year It makes us sound

We need that hope to move around

And when we move from place to place

We see the smile across your face.

6

Why

As I think of the human race

Disappearing without trace

As I think the old, the young

You could too, be the one

We right now, should work together

Before this year is gone forever

The human race is fast still growing

And so the end is us not knowing

Now's the time to make a stand

To help each other to lend a hand

And as I sit I sit I cry

I just think why, why, why

7

Mother's day

On this special caring day

Mothers everywhere will say

This our day, our day of rest

Because we know

You love us best

This goes without say

They are the best in everyway

We love you mothers

Come what may

From us to you this special day

8

Mother's day

On this special caring day

Mothers everywhere will say

This our day, our day of rest

Because we know

You love us best

This goes without say

They are the best in everyway

We love you mothers

Come what may

From us to you this special day

9

Close Friends

With each day we stay inside

We are correct, we do abide

We shed a tear when were apart

The tear that drops is from the heart

With this moment, it's so unfair

We do all this because we care

With each person that's working on

You are the heart were leaning on

When were close but far apart

We love each other and a warming heart

We want to hug, it will trend

As for now, we are close friends.

10

Locked in Time

When one heart beats alone

Love you have, will have grown

When one heart beats along

The love you have is never gone.

When one heart beats with mine

The love you have is locked in time.

When two hearts beat together

The love will stay, will stay forever.

11

We serve, we smile

With each day we serve with trust

The public see us, we are a must

We serve we smile with each day,

The public see us, in a happy way

We serve, we stack we go the extra mile

We do it all, with a smile

With each day lockdown goes on

It knocks us down, but we carry on

We are a store that won't give in

So come on public

Keep Coming in.

12

Angels Falling

Angels falling, worlds apart
Loving feelings from the start

Angels falling, touching skies
Loving families, last goodbyes

Holding hands, keep on trying
Angels falling, people crying

The land we live is green and calling
As from the sky are angels falling

13

Mothers Love

Mothering Sunday comes each year

You are the best, we love you dear

With this Sunday, we want to say

We want to treat you, in every way

You do your best all year round

You do all this, without a sound

Mothers love without knowing

That there loving, is forever growing

Treat your mother so happily

With love and kisses from your family

We trust this day like so many others

We send our love to all our mothers.

14

Time is moving

Time is moving, And wind blows strong

The love for you Now belongs

Time is moving, And the wind blows weak

The love for you, forever seek

Time is moving, And the wind blows

upon the ground

My love for you, I have found

The love for you is forever sound

15

Into the Sun

When the day is full of light

The sun it shines, so very bright

when the sun comes out each day

the joy it brings in every way

when the sun set's each night

it disappears, but what a sight

When we walk, we walk with pride

into the sun we do not hide

So warm, so hot, the heat's the one

As we walk, to carry on

And when the night is dark to see

We bid goodnight for you and me.

16

Sunshine

Sunshine is here to be

You are my love, for me to see

Sunshine and days with you

Lots of sunshine, skies of blue

Sunshine so bright and clear,

you are my Sunshine when you are here

Sunshine is happiness,

love with you, is all the best.

17

We Want to smile

With the face mask we've worn for a while

We need the day, we need that smile

We made the world a safer place

With the mask wrapped round our face

Time has come, to stop feeling blue

To lose the mask and smile at you

We want to smile, for you to see

Without the mask, and feeling free

With the facemask we will Endeavor

To lose the mask, we hope forever

With the facemask we could trace

hang onto it, just in case.

Smile once again

18

Upon a Dream

When you wish upon a dream

You dream a time that could have been

That dream you have may be small

The dream you have is not for all

And the dream you have on this day

Is the dream that comes your way

And when your dream comes to be

The dream you have, is all to see.

19

Beauty Within

Everything changes but beauty remains
with something so tender I can't explain
The beauty I see, comes within
The touch I fill so small, so slim
Beauty a sound so nice to say
I love to speak it every day

Everything changes
Which can make you weep?
But beauty is,
Only skin deep

20

Loving you

Loving you, I want to be

Loving you, is you & me

Loving you, is sweet caress

Loving you, is tenderness

Loving you, through the years

Loving you, warms my tears

Loving you, everyday

Loving you, in everyway

Loving you is,

Loving you

And Loving you

Is all a do.

21

Sleep Loving Angel

It's been some years, since you fell asleep
Tears keep coming, that I want to keep
This is the time to be sincere
With loving kisses we miss you here

With days of past, and on this day
We miss you always in every way
Our Sleeping angel we miss you so dear
Sleeping angel we miss you each year

You are our angel you keep us so close
Why every day, we miss you most
Sleep loving angel at peace with time.

22

Cherished Time

As the time with you is bliss
I catch each moment with a kiss
As each day our lives entwine
To hold you in this cherished time

We take each day so very slow
So our love has time to grow
We toast our love With a glass of wine

And with my glass
full of wine
You are my love
in our cherished time

23

Who can say?

Who can say? What is a crying Heart?
Who can say? What is love?
I can say a crying Heart is love itself

Who can say? When you can dream
Who can say? How long to hold someone
I can say a dream is already happened

Who can say? When to wipe that tear away Who can
say? I love you
I can say let me catch that tear
And say I love you with all my heart

24

I think of you

As I lay upon the sand

I think of you, hand in hand

With your hand, so warm in mine

Holding hands grow old in time

I think of you

when the sun is pleasing

I think of you in a loving reason

I think of you

when it rains, and then goes

when the sun it shines

with a loving rainbow

I think of you

25

Love is coming

Love is coming through my heart

The warmth of love, will never part

With my love is pure desire

Now you set my heart on fire

Love is coming thick & fast

My love for you, will forever last

With the love of ours so sweet

And Velvet kisses when we greet

Love is here and here we play

Loving you in everyday

Lasting love in your eyes

Forever love is no surprise

26

Let love be

The time has come, the sun is shining

The dream of happiness is like velvet lining

The time has come, the sun is hot

The time for love is to love a lot

The time has come, the time to be

The time to love just you and me

The time has come; you are for me

Time to love, and let love be

27

Special wish

When bells ring out a brand new day

The words I have, I need to say

On this very special day

Comes love and happiness in everyway

The words I have, is you in mind

Of words you speak to be so kind

Now this day is so full of love

It makes me think of two white doves

And on this special day like this

A special kiss and make a wish

Now this day is in view

Your special wish Will, come true

28

Kind world

With the world so full of rain

The time has come for us to change

We've seen our land full apart

It would right to make a start

As we leave the world behind

We save our children, it would be kind

The world has seen so much grief

It goes beyond, beyond belief

We need to stop the mess right now

But I don't think, they know how

The world needs to be our friend

Otherwise the world will end

29

Wing of an Angel

When we see an angels wing
We see an angel that may not sing
When we hear an angels voice
Love is the time, to rejoice

When we hear an angel cry
We fill it's time, to say goodbye
And when we see an angel smile
We sit and have a think for a while

And when we find the angels wing
That caring angel begins to sing.

30

Old Hearts

With hearts of old

But young at heart

The dreams we have

Are dreams apart?

With hearts of old

Is loving you

Your heart is young

And so are you

With hearts of old

Sweet and warm

The time we have

Is love reborn

31

What if I told you?

What if I told you, it was all meant to be?
Would you believe me? Would you agree?
What if I told you, love is not to be missed?
Would you hold me?
Would you for ever be kissed?

What if I told you, the look in your eyes?
Reflects our love, and never dies.
What if I told you, is love blind
Love is love however you find.

32

Christmas Time

Christmas is a time of joy

For every girl, & every boy

Christmas is a time of love

For those we see,

and those in heaven above

Christmas is a time, that maybe cold

It's also a time to think of the old

Christmas is a time of hits and misses

And a time of mistletoe kisses.

33

Little children sleep

Christmas time, the man in red

Little children asleep in bed

The sky is dark, the ground is white

Little children pure delight

Christmas time families sings

The joy of carols singing brings

Christmas time, that could be cold

a lonely time, as we grow old

Christmas time of fires burning

Santa's coming children yearning

Little children sleepy eyed

Christmas morning is there surprise.

34

Christmas Chime

Its Christmas magic that make's a sound

Its Christmas time, for all around

We sing our songs of Christmas time

We hear the sounds of Christmas Chime.

The joy we have on Christmas morning

Of boy's & girl's Christmas Yawning

As we hear the Christmas chime

We think of Christmas, lost in time.

This is a year of saddest times

We need the love, of Christmas chime

As this year grinds to an end

Love and kisses we do send.

Happy Christmas

35

With each year's Christmas

With each year that Christmas brings
Family comforts a child sings
With each year that Christmas holds
Books are read story's told

With each year's Christmas day
Watching children laugh and play
As they unwrap, each gift they do get
The joy of Christmas they never forget

With each year's, Christmas day after
Racing toy cars, going faster & faster
With this year's Christmas we may need to weep
As we watch the children as they fall asleep.

ABOUT THE AUTHOR

These are poem's That I write from my life
as I'm growing old. Some are sad, some are
happy and some are from Christmas time
which is how the title was born.
I started writing poems from about 1998,

So I have been writing them for about 23
years and this is my 3rd book. I have written
for friends, family weddings, some one asks
me and I start writing.

Printed in Great Britain
by Amazon

73312078R00031